Note to Librarians, Teachers, and Parents:

Blastoff! Readers are carefully developed by literacy experts and combine standards-based content with developmentally appropriate text.

Level 1 provides the most support through repetition of high-frequency words, light text, predictable sentence patterns, and strong visual support.

Level 2 offers early readers a bit more challenge through varied simple sentences, increased text load, and less repetition of high-frequency words.

Level 3 advances early-fluent readers toward fluency through increased text and concept load, less reliance on visuals, longer sentences, and more literary language.

Level 4 builds reading stamina by providing more text per page, increased use of punctuation, greater variation in sentence patterns, and increasingly challenging vocabulary.

Level 5 encourages children to move from "learning to read" to "reading to learn" by providing even more text, varied writing styles, and less familiar topics.

Whichever book is right for your reader, Blastoff! Readers are the perfect books to build confidence and encourage a love of reading that will last a lifetime!

This edition first published in 2019 by Bellwether Media, Inc.

No part of this publication may be reproduced in whole or in part without written permission of the publisher. For information regarding permission, write to Bellwether Media, Inc., Attention: Permissions Department, 6012 Blue Circle Drive, Minnetonka, MN 55343.

Library of Congress Cataloging-in-Publication Data

Names: Schuetz, Kari, author.
Title: Goby Fish and Snapping Shrimp / by Kari Schuetz.
Description: Minneapolis, MN : Bellwether Media, Inc., [2019] | Series: Blastoff! Readers. Animal Tag Teams | Audience: Ages 5-8. | Audience: K to grade 3. | Includes bibliographical references and index.
Identifiers: LCCN 2018033934 (print) | LCCN 2018034868 (ebook) | ISBN 9781681036854 (ebook) | ISBN 9781626179554 (hardcover : alk. paper)
Subjects: LCSH: Mutualism (Biology)–Juvenile literature. | Gobiidae–Behavior–Juvenile literature. | Snapping shrimps–Behavior–Juvenile literature.
Classification: LCC QL638.G7 (ebook) | LCC QL638.G7 S38 2019 (print) | DDC 577.8/52–dc23
LC record available at https://lccn.loc.gov/2018033934

Text copyright © 2019 by Bellwether Media, Inc. BLASTOFF! READERS and associated logos are trademarks and/or registered trademarks of Bellwether Media, Inc. SCHOLASTIC, CHILDREN'S PRESS, and associated logos are trademarks and/or registered trademarks of Scholastic Inc., 557 Broadway, New York, NY 10012.

Editor: Betsy Rathburn   Designer: Brittany McIntosh

Printed in the United States of America, North Mankato, MN

Table of Contents

Time to Hide	4
Fish Friends	8
Clawed Crustaceans	12
Helping Each Other	16
Glossary	22
To Learn More	23
Index	24

Time to Hide

A goby fish looks after a snapping shrimp. The shrimp cannot see **predators**.

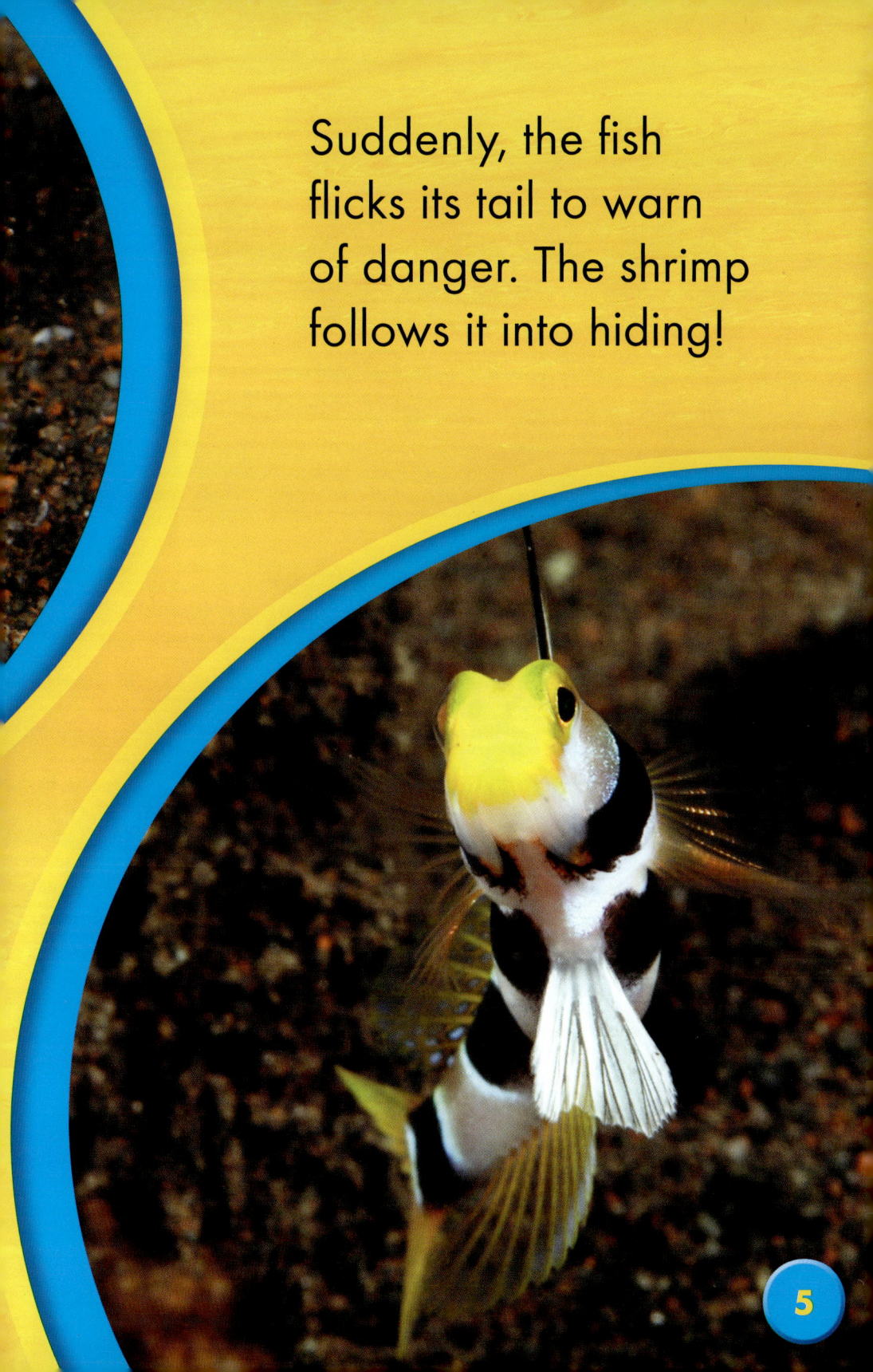

Suddenly, the fish flicks its tail to warn of danger. The shrimp follows it into hiding!

Goby fish and snapping shrimp hang out in **coral reefs**.

These bottom dwellers live together in sandy underwater **burrows**. They use **symbiosis** as a way to stay safe.

Fish Friends

Goby fish are small fish with frog-like faces. They have thick lips and big eyes.

Their long bodies end with rounded tails. Fins on their undersides form **suction cups** to hold the fish in place.

Pink-speckled Shrimpgoby Profile

type: fish
size: up to 6 inches (15 centimeters) long
life span: up to 10 years

Goby fish are **carnivores**. They eat small **invertebrates** that come their way.

burrow

During the day, they attach to **coral** or rock and wait for food. At night, the fish sleep in their burrows.

Clawed Crustaceans

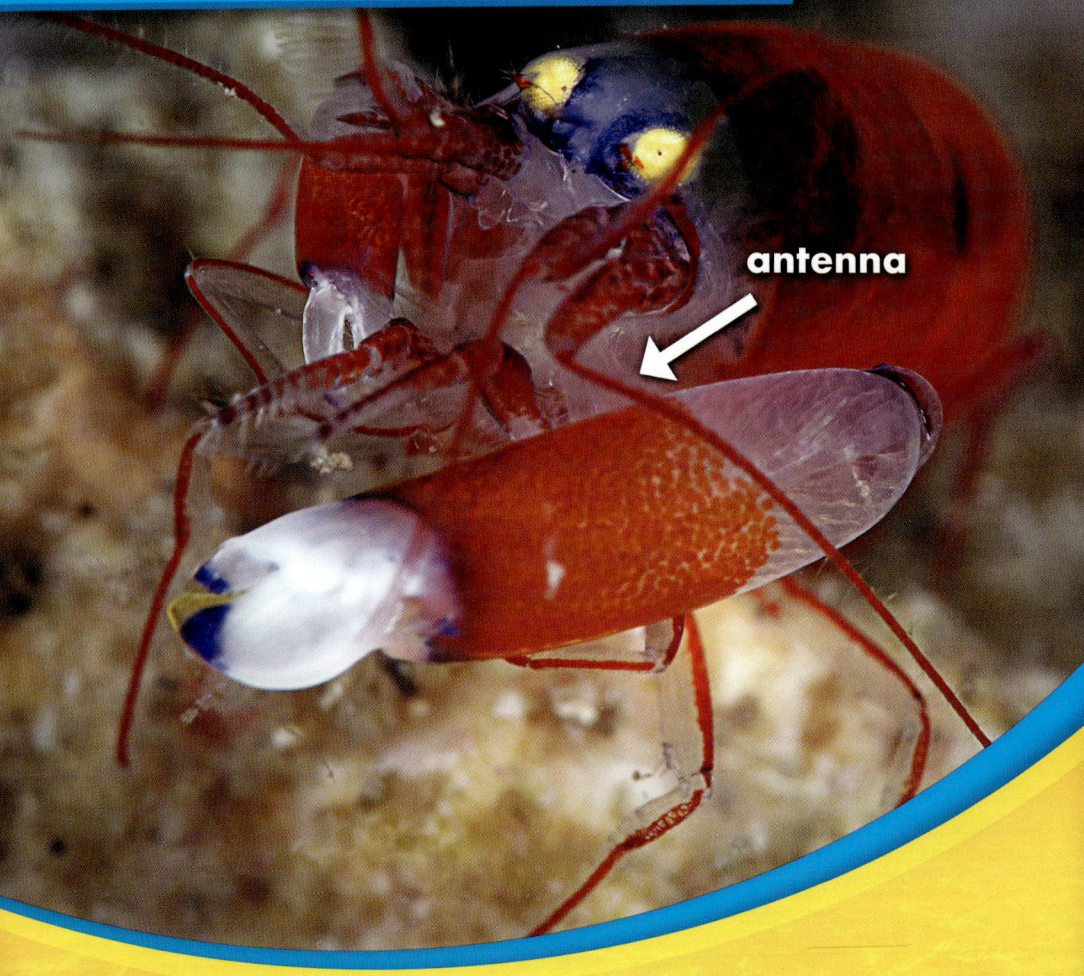

antenna

Snapping shrimp are **crustaceans** with unusual claws. Each shrimp has one small claw and one giant claw.

Long **antennae** help these blind animals feel their way around underwater.

Red-striped Snapping Shrimp Profile

type: crustacean
size: about 1 inch (3 centimeters) long
life span: unknown

To hunt, the shrimp shoot bubbles at their **prey**. They snap their big claws shut to fire bubbles.

Their bubbles make a loud popping sound. They **stun** small fish and other targets!

Helping Each Other

Snapping shrimp let goby fish live in the shrimps' burrows. The fish need places to hide and to lay eggs.

The shrimp need guards to watch over their homes.

These roommates stay together to feed on small fish. The shrimp share leftovers with the gobies.

In return, the fish flip their tails to warn of danger. They help the shrimp escape!

Tag Team Trades

goby fish — watch for danger, give protection

snapping shrimp — provide shelter, provide meals

As partners, goby fish and snapping shrimp take on different roles.

The shrimp dig and fix up burrows. The fish spot danger outside of the home. They succeed as a team!

Glossary

antennae—long, thin feelers that extend from the heads of some animals

burrows—underground homes where some animals live

carnivores—animals that only eat meat

coral—a hard material formed from the skeletons of small animals

coral reefs—coral formations in the ocean, often in warm and shallow waters

crustaceans—animals with hard shells that do not have a backbone

invertebrates—animals that do not have a backbone

predators—animals that hunt other animals for food

prey—animals that are hunted by other animals for food

stun—to make motionless

suction cups—flexible circles that can stick to many surfaces

symbiosis—a close relationship between very different living things

To Learn More

AT THE LIBRARY

Cunningham, Kevin. *Goby Fish and Pistol Shrimp.* Ann Arbor, Mich.: Cherry Lake Publishing, 2017.

Hanáčková, Pavla. *Amazing Animal Friendships: Odd Couples in Nature.* Brighton, England: Salariya, 2017.

Loh-Hagan, Virginia. *Top 10: Partnerships.* Ann Arbor, Mich.: Cherry Lake Publishing, 2017.

ON THE WEB

FACTSURFER

Factsurfer.com gives you a safe, fun way to find more information.

1. Go to www.factsurfer.com.
2. Enter "goby fish and snapping shrimp" into the search box.
3. Click the "Surf" button and select your book cover to see a list of related web sites.

Index

antennae, 12, 13
bodies, 9
bubbles, 14, 15
burrows, 7, 11, 16, 21
carnivores, 10
claws, 12, 14
coral, 11
coral reefs, 6
crustaceans, 12
danger, 5, 19, 21
eggs, 16
eyes, 8
fins, 9
follow, 5
food, 11
hide, 5, 16
hunt, 14
invertebrates, 10
lips, 8
pink-speckled shrimpgoby profile, 9

predators, 4
prey, 14
range, 7
red-striped snapping shrimp profile, 13
stun, 15
suction cups, 9
symbiosis, 7
tail, 5, 9, 19
trades, 19
warn, 5, 19

The images in this book are reproduced through the courtesy of: Song Heming, front cover (goby fish), p. 10; Yann hubert, front cover (snapping shrimp); Mirko Zanni/ Getty Images, pp. 4, 5; cbimages/ Alamy, pp. 6-7, 11, 21; Marli Wakeling/ Alamy, p. 8; Audrey R. Smith, p. 9; RibeirodosSantos, p. 12; Joel Sartore, National Geographic Photo Ark/ Getty Images, p. 13; Stocktrek Images, Inc./ Alamy, pp. 14, 19 (right); Underwater Imaging/ Alamy, p. 15; Richardom/ Alamy, p. 16; David Fleetham/ Alamy, p. 17; Reinhard Dirscherl/ Alamy, p. 18; LIN TE-WEI, p. 19 (left); Scubazoo/ SuperStock, p. 20.